TOSEL®
READING SERIES

JUNIOR

READING

2

ITC International TOSEL Committee

CONTENTS

About TOSEL®

TOSEL (Test of Skills in the English Language) was developed to meet the demand for a more effective assessment of English as a foreign language for learners from specific cultural settings.

TOSEL evaluates and certifies the proficiency levels of English learners, from the age of 4 through adulthood, along with academic and job performance results.

Background

- Other English tests are ineffective in accurately measuring individual abilities
- Overuse of US-dominated testing systems in diverse cultural and educational contexts in the global English language learning market

Functions & Usage

- Assessment is categorized into 7 levels
- Used as a qualification for academic excellence for school admissions
- Used as a test to assess the English proficiency in the corporate and public sectors

Goals

- Create an effective tool for assessing and evaluating the English skills of English language learners
- Implement efficient and accessible testing systems and methods
- Provide constructive and developmental English education guidance

TOSEL® Strength

LEVELED ASSESSMENTS

An established English test system fit for seven different levels according to learners' cognitive development

ACCURATE DIAGNOSIS

A systematic and scientific diagnosis of learners' English proficiency

EXTENSIVE MATERIALS

Supplementary materials to help learners in an EFL environment to prepare for TOSEL and improve their proficiency

SUFFICIENT DATA

Content for each level developed by using data accumulated from more than 2,000,000 TOSEL test takers delegated at 15,000 schools and academies

CLASSIFIED AREAS OF INTELLIGENCE

Content designed to foster and expand the strengths of each student, categorized by the eight areas of intelligence

CONTINUITY

A complete course of English education ranging from kindergarten, elementary school, middle school, high schoool, and up to adults.

HIGH RELIABILITY

A high reliability level (Cronbach's alpha: .904 for elementary school students / .864 for university students) proven by several studies (Oxford University / Modern Language Journal)

SYSTEMATIC & EFFECTIVE ENGLISH EDUCATION

Accurate diagnosis and extensive materials which provide a step-by-step development in English learning, according to the quality of each learner's ability

TOSEL® Level Chart

Seven Separate Assessments

TOSEL divides the test into seven stages, by considering the test takers' cognitive levels, according to different ages. Unlike other assessments based on only one level, TOSEL includes separate assessments for preschool, elementary school, middle school, high school students, and for adults, which also includes both professionals and college students.

TOSEL's reporting system highlights the strengths and weaknesses of each test taker and suggests areas for further development.

COCOON

Suitable for children aged 4-6 (pre-schoolers)

The first step in the TOSEL system, the test is composed of colorful designs and interesting questions to interest young learners and to put them at ease.

Pre-STARTER

Suitable for children aged 7-8 (1st-2nd grades of elementary school)

Evaluates the ability to comprehend simple vocabulary, conversations, and sentences.

STARTER

Suitable for children aged 9-10 (3rd-4th grades of elementary school)

Evaluates the ability to comprehend short sentences and conversations related to everyday situations or topics.

BASIC

Suitable for children aged 11-12 (5th–6th grades of elementary school)

Evaluates the ability to communicate about personal information, daily activities, future plans, and past experiences in written and spoken language.

JUNIOR

Suitable for middle school students

Evaluates the ability to comprehend short paragraphs, practical texts, and speech covering general topics and to participate in simple daily conversations.

HIGH JUNIOR

Suitable for high school students

Evaluates the ability to use English fluently, accurately, and effectively on a wide range of social and academic subjects, as well as the ability to use sentences with a variety of complex structures.

ADVANCED

Suitable for university students and adults

Evaluates the ability to use practical English required for a job or work environment, as well as the ability to use and understand English at the university level.

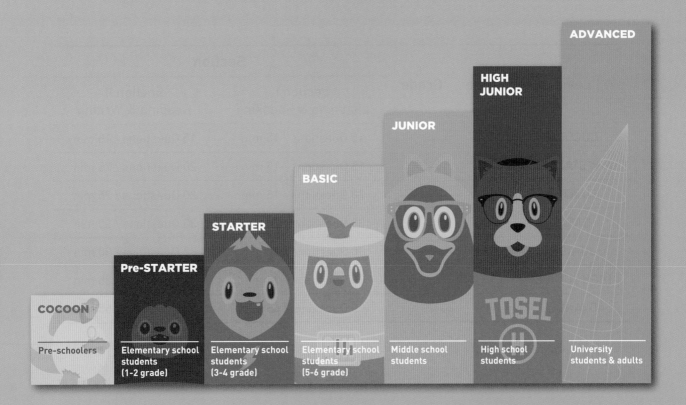

COCOON — Pre-schoolers

Pre-STARTER — Elementary school students (1-2 grade)

STARTER — Elementary school students (3-4 grade)

BASIC — Elementary school students (5-6 grade)

JUNIOR — Middle school students

HIGH JUNIOR — High school students

ADVANCED — University students & adults

TOSEL

Evaluation

Assessing the Four Skills

TOSEL evaluates the four language skills: reading, listening, speaking and writing, through indirect and direct assessment items.

This system of evaluation is part of a concerted effort to break away from materials geared solely toward grammar and reading-oriented education.

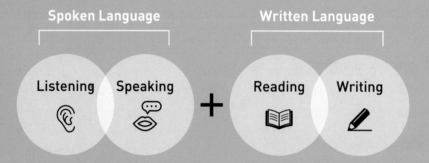

TOSEL Test Information

Level	Score	Grade	Section	
			Section I Listening & Speaking	Section II Reading & Writing
COCOON	100		15 Questions / 15 min	15 Questions / 15 min
Pre-STARTER	100		15 Questions / 15 min	20 Questions / 25 min
STARTER	100		20 Questions / 15 min	20 Questions / 25 min
BASIC	100	1-10	30 Questions / 20 min	30 Questions / 30 min
JUNIOR	100		30 Questions / 20 min	30 Questions / 30 min
HIGH JUNIOR	100		30 Questions / 25 min	35 Questions / 35 min
ADVANCED	990		70 Questions / 45 min	70 Questions / 55 min

Certificates

TOSEL Certificate

The International TOSEL Committee officially evaluates and certifies the level of English proficiency of English learners from the age of 4 to adults.

Certified by

Mar. 2010	Korea University
Dec. 2009	The Korean Society of Speech Science
Dec. 2009	The Korea Association of Foreign Language Education
Nov. 2009	The Applied Linguistics Association of Korea
Oct. 2009	The Pan Korea English Teachers Association

CHAPTER 1

Sports

Teacher's Book
p.106

UNIT 1

Sit-ups

Do you exercise regularly? What kind of exercise do you do?

Many sports programs include sit-ups. Sometimes schools even test students on their ability to do many sit-ups. However, sit-ups are not always safe to do. If you do not do sit-ups properly, you can get an injury. Therefore, when you do a sit-up, you should follow six key steps. First, bend your knees, and put your heels and feet flat on the ground. Next, cross your arms across your chest. After that, tighten your stomach muscles. Try to get your belly-button close to your spine. Next, with your heels and toes flat on the ground, gently lift your head first and your shoulders next. Look at your knees. Now you are sitting up. Stay here for a moment. Then, lower your back close to the ground. However, you must remember something important here. You must not bring your back all the way to the ground. Instead, you must keep your back slightly above the ground. Using this proper form to do sit-ups can help you strengthen your stomach muscles and prevent injuries.

New Words

sit-up

n a type of exercise meant to make stronger muscles near the stomach

injury

n a place where you are hurt

heel

n the back part of a foot

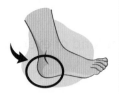

cross your arms

v fold your arms

lower X

v make X less high

strengthen X

v to make X stronger

Part A. Sentence Completion

1. A: How _____ chin-ups can you do in a minute?
   B: Maybe just three.

   (A) long
   (B) large
   (C) much
   (D) many

2. A: Can you show me _____ sit-ups?
   B: Alright. First, bend your knees.

   (A) how do to
   (B) how to do
   (C) to do how
   (D) to how do

Part B. Situational Writing

3.

My friend is over there. Her _____.

   (A) legs are bent
   (B) eyes are closed
   (C) knees are raised
   (D) arms are crossed

4.

He has a foot _____.

   (A) bath
   (B) injury
   (C) doctor
   (D) powder

Muscles-R-Us Gym

Want muscles? Want strength?
Come to Muscles-R-Us Gym!

We have coaches for personal training.
We have amazing machines.
We have the latest technology.
We can teach you the proper exercise form.

Monthly memberships: $ 20.00
Yearly memberships: $ 220.00

What are you waiting for? Join Muscles-R-Us today!

5. Which is NOT offered at Muscles-R-Us?

(A) group classes
(B) excellent machines
(C) one-on-one coaching
(D) up-to-date technology

6. How much can users save over 12 months paying yearly instead of monthly?

(A) $10.00
(B) $20.00
(C) $30.00
(D) $40.00

Part D. General Reading and Retelling

Many sports programs include sit-ups. Sometimes schools even test students on their ability to do many sit-ups. However, sit-ups are not always safe to do. If you do not do sit-ups properly, you can get an injury. Therefore, when you do a sit-up, you should follow six key steps. First, bend your knees, and put your heels and feet flat on the ground. Next, cross your arms across your chest. After that, tighten your stomach muscles. Try to get your belly-button close to your spine. Next, with your heels and toes flat on the ground, gently lift your head first and your shoulders next. Look at your knees. Now you are sitting up. Stay here for a moment. Then, lower your back close to the ground. However, you must remember something important here. You must not bring your back all the way to the ground. Instead, you must keep your back slightly above the ground. Using this proper form to do sit-ups can help you strengthen your stomach muscles and prevent injuries.

7. Which of the following is the best title for the passage?

   (A) Dealing with Back Injuries
   (B) Improving Health at Schools
   (C) The Right Way to Do a Sit-up
   (D) Why Students Need More Exercise

8. According to the passage, where should your feet go?

   (A) flat on the ground
   (B) straight out in front
   (C) over a crossed knee
   (D) shoulder-width apart

9. What does the passage say NOT to do?

   (A) cross your arms
   (B) look at your knees
   (C) tighten your stomach muscles
   (D) let your back touch the ground

10. Which of the following people would most likely benefit from the advice?

   (A) someone with a broken back
   (B) someone aiming for thinner legs
   (C) someone trying to get smoother skin
   (D) someone wanting strong stomach muscles

Listening Practice

 Listen and write.

  MP3 J2-1

Sit-ups

Many sports programs include ¹ _____ . Sometimes schools even test students on their ability to do many sit-ups. However, sit-ups are not always safe to do. If you do not do sit-ups properly, you can get an ² _____ . Therefore, when you do a sit-up, you should follow six key steps. First, bend your knees, and put your ³ _____ and feet flat on the ground. Next, ⁴ _____ your arms across your chest. After that, tighten your stomach muscles. Try to get your belly-button close to your spine. Next, with your heels and toes flat on the ground, gently lift your head first and your shoulders next. Look at your knees. Now you are sitting up. Stay here for a moment. Then, ⁵ _____ your back close to the ground. However, you must remember something important here. You must not bring your back all the way to the ground. Instead, you must keep your back slightly above the ground. Using this proper form to do sit-ups can help you ⁶ _____ your stomach muscles and prevent injuries.

Word Bank

hills	sit-ups	injery
sit-up	closs	louer
injury	strengten	cross
heels	lower	strengthen

 Listen. Pause. Say each sentence.

  MP3 J2-1G

Writing Practice

 Write the words.

1 _____

n a type of exercise meant to make stronger muscles near the stomach

2 _____

n a place where you are hurt

3 _____

 n the back part of a foot

4 _____

v fold your arms

5 _____ X

v make X less high

6 _____ X

v to make X stronger

📄 **Write the words in each blank.**

Summary

Sit-ups are not always _____ to do and can cause injuries. Therefore, you should follow the right way to do _____. This can help you _____ your stomach muscles and _____ injuries.

Word Puzzle

 Complete the word puzzle.

1 ↓ a place where you are hurt

3 → a type of exercise meant to make stronger muscles near the stomach

2 ↓ fold your arms

4 → make X less high

3 ↓ to make X stronger

5 → the back part of a foot

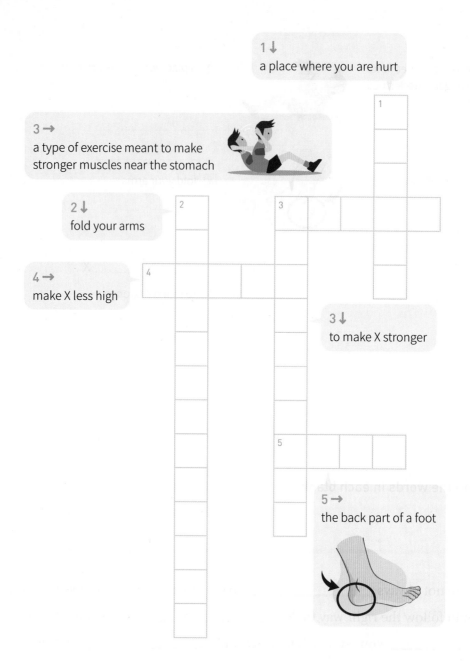

Teacher's Book p.110

UNIT 2

The Skeleton

Are there any winter sports that you enjoy watching or playing?

One exciting winter Olympics sport is the skeleton. The skeleton is known for its fast pace and up-to-date technology. Interestingly, even a long time ago, this sport's technology was modern and fast. In 1882, some men from England were in Switzerland. They made a huge ice track in Switzerland. The track led from one town to another town. Back then, cold countries had many tracks like this big one. However, the new track in Switzerland had something special: curves. For a long time in history, people used wooden sleds. Therefore, people used wooden sleds to go down the tracks in Switzerland, too. Then one day, Mr. Child, an Englishman, came to the tracks. Instead of a wooden sled, he used one that was mostly made of metal. The metal sled was very sturdy and fast. How did that metal sled get the name "skeleton"? Maybe it looked a little like a skeleton. Or maybe it was based on a word from Norway: "Kjaelke." It is not sure what the name means. But we do know that Mr. Child's sled helped lead to the modern, dangerous Olympic sport of the skeleton.

New Words

track *n* a type of path	**curve** *n* a line that is not straight
sled *n* a type of wooden or metal cart that slides on ice or snow	**be made of** *v* be constructed out of
sturdy *adj* strong	**skeleton** *n* ① the bones of a human body ② a winter sport

Part A. Sentence Completion

1. A: Do you play a lot of computer games?
    B: Yes. My favorite is one _____ "Speed Cars."

    (A) called
    (B) to call
    (C) calling
    (D) be called

2. A: Do you have a metal desk?
    B: No, my desk is made _____ wood.

    (A) at
    (B) in
    (C) of
    (D) for

Part B. Situational Writing

3.

    There are three horses on the _____.

    (A) boat
    (B) track
    (C) road
    (D) truck

4.

    There is a _____ in the road.

    (A) can
    (B) curve
    (C) cyclist
    (D) cactus

For Sale: Antique Wooden Sled

- Probably made in the 1890s
- From the New York area
- Still has the original red paint
- Made with square nails
- 30cm wide
- Similar to sleds featured in paintings by Brantio
- No longer safe to ride downhill

$349.99 (pick up at my office in Boston only)

$46.45 shipping (within the US and Canada only)

5. Which of the following is mentioned about the sled?

(A) how wide it is
(B) how fast it goes
(C) the exact year it was made
(D) the name of the original owner

6. Who would most likely buy the sled?

(A) someone who adores the color pink
(B) someone who likes to look at old objects
(C) someone who wants to go fast down a slope
(D) someone whose shipping address is in Norway

Part D. General Reading and Retelling

One exciting winter Olympics sport is the skeleton. The skeleton is known for its fast pace and up-to-date technology. Interestingly, even a long time ago, this sport's technology was modern and fast. In 1882, some men from England were in Switzerland. They made a huge ice track in Switzerland. The track led from one town to another town. Back then, cold countries had many tracks like this big one. However, the new track in Switzerland had something special: curves. For a long time in history, people used wooden sleds. Therefore, people used wooden sleds to go down the tracks in Switzerland, too. Then one day, Mr. Child, an Englishman, came to the tracks. Instead of a wooden sled, he used one that was mostly made of metal. The metal sled was very sturdy and fast. How did that metal sled get the name "skeleton"? Maybe it looked a little like a skeleton. Or maybe it was based on a word from Norway: "Kjaelke." It is not sure what the name means. But we do know that Mr. Child's sled helped lead to the modern, dangerous Olympic sport of the skeleton.

7. What is the passage mainly about?

(A) how the skeleton developed as a sport
(B) the most dangerous skeleton race of all time
(C) which countries win the most skeleton races
(D) the years the Olympics included the skeleton

8. According to the passage, who made a huge ice track in Switzerland?

(A) Mr. Child
(B) some English men
(C) a man from Norway
(D) some Swiss soldiers

9. According to the passage, how did Mr. Child make his sled different from traditional ones?

(A) He made the sides thinner.
(B) He put a motor on the front.
(C) He painted it in Olympic colors.
(D) He included mainly metal parts.

10. According to the passage, where did the name "skeleton" come from?

(A) A sled was made of animal bones.
(B) Sleds used to have white decorations.
(C) It was based on a word from Switzerland.
(D) No one is certain where the name came from.

Listening Practice

 Listen and write.

  MP3 J2-2

The Skeleton

One exciting winter Olympics sport is the skeleton. The skeleton is known for its fast pace and up-to-date technology. Interestingly, even a long time ago, this sport's technology was modern and fast. In 1882, some men from England were in Switzerland. They made a huge ice ¹_____ in Switzerland. The track led from one town to another town. Back then, cold countries had many tracks like this big one.

However, the new track in Switzerland had something special: ²_____. For a long time in history, people used wooden ³_____. Therefore, people used wooden sleds to go down the tracks in Switzerland, too. Then one day, Mr. Child, an Englishman, came to the tracks. Instead of a wooden sled, he used one that was mostly ⁴_____ metal. The metal sled was very ⁵_____ and fast. How did that metal sled get the name "skeleton"? Maybe it looked a little like a ⁶_____. Or maybe it was based on a word from Norway: "Kjaelke." It is not sure what the name means. But we do know that Mr. Child's sled helped lead to the modern, dangerous Olympic sport of the skeleton.

Word Bank

curbes	skeleton	stirdy
skelton	sturdy	sleds
made of	trak	curves
sled	madeof	track

 Listen. Pause. Say each sentence.

  MP3 J2-2G

Writing Practice

ABC **Write the words.**

1 _____

n a type of path

2 _____

n a line that is not straight

3 _____

n a type of wooden or metal cart that slides on ice or snow

4 _____

v be constructed out of

5 _____

adj strong

6 _____

n ① the bones of a human body
② a winter sport

Write the words in each blank.

Summary

The exciting _____ winter sport of skeleton has always used modern, fast

_____. In 1882, an Englishman used a sled mostly made of _____

instead of wood. His sled helped the development of modern _____.

Word Puzzle

Complete the word puzzle.

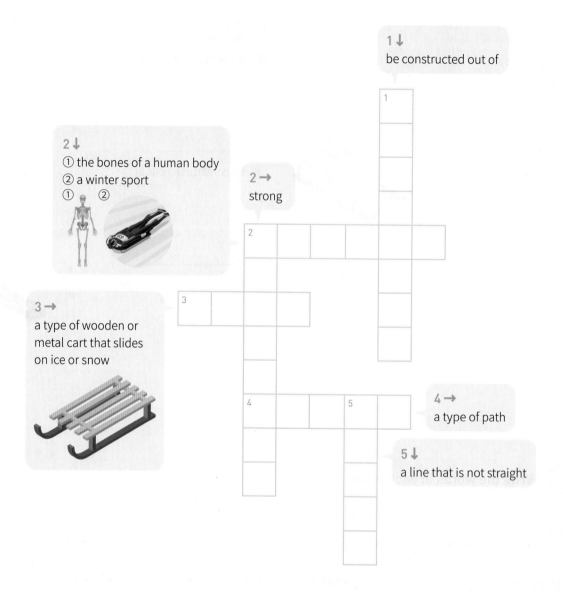

1 ↓
be constructed out of

2 ↓
① the bones of a human body
② a winter sport
①   ②

2 →
strong

3 →
a type of wooden or metal cart that slides on ice or snow

4 →
a type of path

5 ↓
a line that is not straight

Teacher's Book
p.115

UNIT 3

Doping in Sports

List three rules that apply to all sports.

Doping is when athletes take illegal drugs to perform better in their sport. Doping is so common that a special group called the World Anti-Doping Agency (WADA) checks for doping cases. According to one WADA study, more than 40% of world championship athletes have used doping substances. Athletes who get caught doping may be prohibited from competing again. Doping is cheating, and it is terrible for athletes' bodies. So why do some athletes choose to dope? The obvious answer is because they want to win. But a closer look at the issue reveals other reasons related to winning. For example, in some sports, top players are already doping when new athletes join the sport. To be able to compete at the same level, some athletes may feel they need to dope, too. For example, in some years of the Tour de France bicycle race, it was found that all the top cyclists were doping. Another reason could be because some sports involve a lot of money. Some athletes may worry that without doping, they will lose their contracts. Whatever the reason, any athlete considering doping should know that it is cheating.

New Words

doping

n using drugs that are not allowed in a sport

illegal

adj against the law

be prohibited from

v be not allowed to do

related to

adj connected to

cheating

n breaking the rules

contract

n an official deal

Part A. **Sentence Completion**

1. A: Why _____ some athletes break the rules?
    B: Maybe they feel too much pressure.

    (A) do
    (B) has
    (C) does
    (D) have

2. A: _____ the cyclists in this race are 15 years old.
    B: So they're teenagers.

    (A) All
    (B) None
    (C) Much
    (D) Every

Part B. **Situational Writing**

3.

    Paul is _____.

    (A) cheating on a test
    (B) standing on a desk
    (C) holding his friend's hand
    (D) being watched by Mr. wei

4.

    Dogs are _____ here.

    (A) allowed
    (B) popular
    (C) welcome
    (D) prohibited

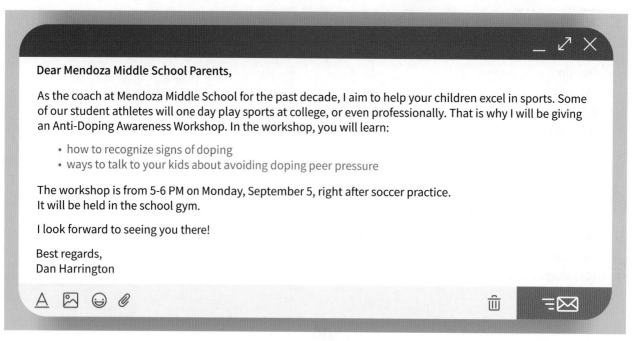

Dear Mendoza Middle School Parents,

As the coach at Mendoza Middle School for the past decade, I aim to help your children excel in sports. Some of our student athletes will one day play sports at college, or even professionally. That is why I will be giving an Anti-Doping Awareness Workshop. In the workshop, you will learn:

- how to recognize signs of doping
- ways to talk to your kids about avoiding doping peer pressure

The workshop is from 5-6 PM on Monday, September 5, right after soccer practice. It will be held in the school gym.

I look forward to seeing you there!

Best regards,
Dan Harrington

5. Who is Dan Harrington?

(A) a school principal
(B) a leader of WADA
(C) a middle school coach
(D) a Mendoza city police officer

6. What can attendees do at the workshop?

(A) meet a professional basketball star
(B) get to know a school's new soccer coach
(C) learn about ways of talking about peer pressure
(D) see their children play against a competing school

Part D. General Reading and Retelling

Doping is when athletes take illegal drugs to perform better in their sport. Doping is so common that a special group called the World Anti-Doping Agency (WADA) checks for doping cases. According to one WADA study, more than 40% of world championship athletes have used doping substances. Athletes who get caught doping may be prohibited from competing again. Doping is cheating, and it is terrible for athletes' bodies. So why do some athletes choose to dope? The obvious answer is because they want to win. But a closer look at the issue reveals other reasons related to winning. For example, in some sports, top players are already doping when new athletes join the sport. To be able to compete at the same level, some athletes may feel they need to dope, too. For example, in some years of the Tour de France bicycle race, it was found that all the top cyclists were doping. Another reason could be because some sports involve a lot of money. Some athletes may worry that without doping, they will lose their contracts. Whatever the reason, any athlete considering doping should know that it is cheating.

7. Which is the best title for the passage?

   (A) Reasons Why Athletes Dope
   (B) Why We Cannot Catch Dopers
   (C) How the World Stopped Doping
   (D) Joining the World Anti-Doping Agency

8. According to the passage, how many world championship athletes have tried doping?

   (A) less than 20%
   (B) about 30%
   (C) over 40%
   (D) just under 60%

9. What is NOT a reason for doping mentioned in the passage?

   (A) wanting to win
   (B) enjoying taking risks
   (C) worrying about losing money
   (D) competing at the same level as dopers

10. What would the writer most likely say to an athlete who wants to dope?

   (A) "That will be safe."
   (B) "That would be cheating."
   (C) "That is not my business."
   (D) "That is probably fine for your body."

Listening Practice

 Listen and write.

  MP3 J2-3

Doping in Sports

Doping is when athletes take ¹ _____ drugs to perform better in their sport. Doping is so common that a special group called the World Anti-Doping Agency (WADA) checks for doping cases. According to one WADA study, more than 40% of world championship athletes have used doping substances. Athletes who get caught ² _____ may be ³ _____ from competing again. Doping is ⁴ _____ , and it is terrible for athletes' bodies. So why do some athletes choose to dope? The obvious answer is because they want to win. But a closer look at the issue reveals other reasons ⁵ _____ to winning. For example, in some sports, top players are already doping when new athletes join the sport. To be able to compete at the same level, some athletes may feel they need to dope, too. For example, in some years of the Tour de France bicycle race, it was found that all the top cyclists were doping. Another reason could be because some sports involve a lot of money.

Some athletes may worry that without doping, they will lose their ⁶ _____ . Whatever the reason, any athlete considering doping should know that it is cheating.

Word Bank

conteracts	contracts	related
ilegal	Doping	cheeting
doping	cheating	illegal
relating	prohibit	prohibited

 Listen. Pause. Say each sentence.

  MP3 J2-3G

Writing Practice

 Write the words.

1 _____

n using drugs that are not allowed in a sport

2 _____

adj against the law

3 _____

v be not allowed to do

4 _____

adj connected to

5 _____

n breaking the rules

6 _____

n an official deal

 Write the words in each blank.

Summary

Doping is when athletes take illegal _____ to perform better in their sport. Athletes give various _____ for doping. Whatever the reason, any _____ considering doping should know that it is _____.

Word Puzzle

Complete the word puzzle.

1 ↓
breaking the rules

2 ↓
be not allowed to do

5 ↓
using drugs that
are not allowed
in a sport

3 ↓
an official deal

4 →
connected to

6 →
against the law

Teacher's Book
p.120

UNIT 4

Supersuits

Some swimsuits help swimmers go faster.
Should these swimsuits be allowed in sports competitions?

How much of an athlete's performance comes from strength and ability? How much comes from technology? In 2008 and 2009, these questions became very important in the sport of swimming. In those years, swimmers broke many records in competition. They broke world records at the Olympics and at swimming championships. But the swimmers were wearing special swimsuits. The swimsuits were made of high-performance material. This material made the swimmers lighter in the water. The swimsuits also covered a large part of the body, which helped the swimmers move forward quickly. The swimsuits were completely legal. The swimmers did not break any rules when they wore the suits. However, some critics said these "supersuits" were unfair. In 2010, the swimsuits were banned in major competitions. Now there are more rules about swimsuit material and swimsuit length in competitions. People have started calling the years of 2008 and 2009 the "supersuit era." Some people worry that the records set during the "supersuit era" will never be broken.

New Words

break a record
v perform the best of all time

competition
n a contest or race

high-performance
adj better or faster than others

material
n the stuff that clothes are made from

cover X
v go over X to hide it

ban X
v say that X is not allowed

Part A. Sentence Completion

1. A: One kid said a bad word in class, and we all got punished.
   B: That is so _____!

   (A) unfair
   (B) unfairly
   (C) unfairily
   (D) unfairness

2. A: Have you heard of that swimmer?
   B: Yes. Didn't she _____ a world record?

   (A) break
   (B) broke
   (C) broken
   (D) to break

Part B. Situational Writing

3.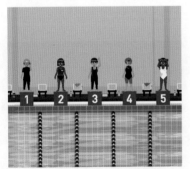

   There are five kids in _____.

   (A) flippers
   (B) each lane
   (C) lifejackets
   (D) the competition

4.

   Calculators are _____ in this class.

   (A) used
   (B) created
   (C) banned
   (D) donated

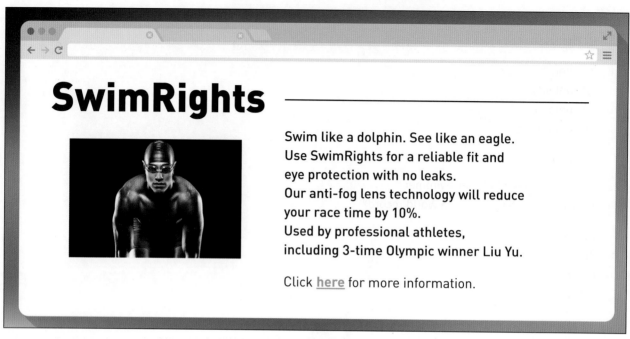

SwimRights

Swim like a dolphin. See like an eagle.
Use SwimRights for a reliable fit and
eye protection with no leaks.
Our anti-fog lens technology will reduce
your race time by 10%.
Used by professional athletes,
including 3-time Olympic winner Liu Yu.

Click **here** for more information.

5.   What is this advertisement most likely for?

(A)   swimsuits
(B)   swim caps
(C)   swim goggles
(D)   swimming ear plugs

6.   What does the ad promise?

(A)   a personalized fitting
(B)   a similar race time to Liu Yu
(C)   a faster time in competitions
(D)   a lower price than other brands

Part D. General Reading and Retelling

How much of an athlete's performance comes from strength and ability? How much comes from technology? In 2008 and 2009, these questions became very important in the sport of swimming. In those years, swimmers broke many records in competition. They broke world records at the Olympics and at swimming championships. But the swimmers were wearing special swimsuits. The swimsuits were made of high-performance material. This material made the swimmers lighter in the water. The swimsuits also covered a large part of the body, which helped the swimmers move forward quickly. The swimsuits were completely legal. The swimmers did not break any rules when they wore the suits. However, some critics said these "supersuits" were unfair. In 2010, the swimsuits were banned in major competitions. Now there are more rules about swimsuit material and swimsuit length in competitions. People have started calling the years of 2008 and 2009 the "supersuit era." Some people worry that the records set during the "supersuit era" will never be broken.

7. What is the passage mainly about?

(A) swimming robots
(B) disabled swimmers
(C) advanced swimsuits
(D) Olympic swimming dates

8. According to the passage, what did the supersuits do in 2008 and 2009?

(A) cover the faces of swimmers
(B) help swimmers escape sharks
(C) protect swimmers from sunburn
(D) make swimmers lighter in the water

9. According to the passage, what happened in 2010?

(A) Supersuits became legal.
(B) Supersuits sold out in stores.
(C) People first bought supersuits online.
(D) Major competitions banned supersuits.

10. According to the passage, what worries some people?

(A) that the Olympics will not have swimming events
(B) that people will stop being interested in swimming
(C) that stopping supersuits will stop human greatness
(D) that future swimmers will never break supersuit era records

Listening Practice

 Listen and write.

  MP3 J2-4

Supersuits

How much of an athlete's performance comes from strength and ability? How much comes from technology? In 2008 and 2009, these questions became very important in the sport of swimming. In those years, swimmers broke many ¹ _____ in ² _____ . They broke world records at the Olympics and at swimming championships. But the swimmers were wearing special swimsuits. The swimsuits were made of ³ _____ material. This ⁴ _____ made the swimmers lighter in the water. The swimsuits also ⁵ _____ a large part of the body, which helped the swimmers move forward quickly. The swimsuits were completely legal. The swimmers did not break any rules when they wore the suits. However, some critics said these "supersuits" were unfair. In 2010, the swimsuits were ⁶ _____ in major competitions. Now there are more rules about swimsuit material and swimsuit length in competitions. People have started calling the years of 2008 and 2009 the "supersuit era." Some people worry that the records set during the "supersuit era" will never be broken.

Word Bank

covers	matirial	recods
high-performance	covered	high-preformance
material	competition	banned
records	ban	compitition

 Listen. Pause. Say each sentence.

  MP3 J2-4G

Writing Practice

 Write the words.

1 _____

v perform the best of all time

2 _____

n a contest or race

3 _____

adj better or faster than others

4 _____

n the stuff that clothes are made from

5 _____ X

v go over X to hide it

6 _____ X

v say that X is not allowed

 Write the words in each blank.

Summary

In 2008 and 2009, swimmers who _____ many records were wearing special swimsuits made of high-performance _____. The swimsuits were legal but some people said they were _____. Now there are more rules about _____ in competitions.

Word Puzzle

Complete the word puzzle.

1 ↓
better or faster than others

2 ↓
go over X to hide it

3 ↓
the stuff that clothes are made from

5 ↓
a contest or race

4 →
perform the best of all time

6 →
say that X is not allowed

A Criminal Catcher

Teacher's Book
p.125

In 1887, people in Toronto, Canada were extremely excited that the city had won its first major baseball championship. However, what many people in the city did not know was that one of the star players, catcher Harry Decker, was a criminal.

Decker came from Chicago, in the U.S. It was in that city that he committed many of his crimes. Most of his crimes were about money. For example, he would sign fake names on money checks. He tried making fake dollar bills. He stole from his teammates. He had many different fake names. Usually, he would find a way to avoid jail. One time, he told the judge that he made mistakes because he had hit his head playing baseball.

Decker did not play long for Toronto's baseball team. It was true that he was skilled. He had even created an important invention — the catcher's mitt. However, his criminal past became known and teams wanted to avoid him. But he became very famous among baseball fans because of his strange past.

CHAPTER 2

Art

UNIT 5

Camera Shots

Teacher's Book
p.126

Movie shots are like pictures in movies.
What movie shots can you remember?

Many film viewers know about sound techniques and lighting techniques in movies. But they may not think about the camera shots. A camera shot is the amount of space that a viewer can see at one time on the screen. There are six main types of camera shot. An "extreme long shot" shows a movie's landscape. It is often used at the beginning of the movie to show the main location. A "long shot" shows a smaller part of the location of the movie. It may show a building, for example. A "full shot" shows the characters. In a full shot, viewers can see the actors' costumes. This shot helps to show relationships. A "mid-shot" shows people from the waist to the head. It is also called a "social shot," because it shows people talking. A "close-up" shows just one character's face. This shot is also called a "personal shot," because it helps show a character's emotions. An "extreme close-up" shows just one part of a face or object. Horror movies sometimes use this technique because it is very intense. These six camera shots help filmmakers tell their stories.

New Words

lighting

n the way that lights are set up

technique

n special way to do something

landscape

n a wide view of a place

location

n a place

costume

n the special clothes that an actor wears

waist

n the part of the body above the hips and below the chest

Part A. Sentence Completion

1. A: How did you learn how to use a camera?
    B: I taught _____. It took a few years.

    (A) my
    (B) me
    (C) mine
    (D) myself

2. A: Which movie is better out of these two choices?
    B: This _____. It uses many interesting camera shots.

    (A) it
    (B) its
    (C) one
    (D) ones

Part B. Situational Writing

3.

This photo shows a natural green _____.

(A) portrait
(B) blanket
(C) costume
(D) landscape

4.

This green dress has a nice bit of black at the _____.

(A) hips
(B) waist
(C) bottom
(D) sleeves

UNIT 5   Camera Shots

When you take the shot, ask yourself these questions:

1. Is there balance? The distance from the forehead to the top of the screen should be equal to the distance from the mouth to the bottom of the screen.

2. Did you use a tri-pod? Without a tri-pod, your camera could shake. You need a clear shot, not a blurry one.

3. Is the image simple? Complicated images are distracting to the eye.

5. What would be the best title of the list?

(A) How to Take a Close-up Shot
(B) Bringing Black and White Film Back
(C) How Animal and Human Shots Differ
(D) Breathing Techniques for Photography

6. Which of the following is NOT mentioned?

(A) achieving simplicity
(B) maintaining balance
(C) choosing filter types
(D) keeping images clear

Many film viewers know about sound techniques and lighting techniques in movies. But they may not think about the camera shots. A camera shot is the amount of space that a viewer can see at one time on the screen. There are six main types of camera shot. An "extreme long shot" shows a movie's landscape. It is often used at the beginning of the movie to show the main location. A "long shot" shows a smaller part of the location of the movie. It may show a building, for example. A "full shot" shows the characters. In a full shot, viewers can see the actors' costumes. This shot helps to show relationships. A "mid-shot" shows people from the waist to the head. It is also called a "social shot," because it shows people talking. A "close-up" shows just one character's face. This shot is also called a "personal shot," because it helps show a character's emotions. An "extreme close-up" shows just one part of a face or object. Horror movies sometimes use this technique because it is very intense. These six camera shots help filmmakers tell their stories.

7. Which is the best title for the passage?

(A) Choosing the Ideal Camera
(B) How to Take Nature Photos
(C) The Six Main Types of Camera Shot
(D) Sound and Lighting Techniques in Film

8. According to the passage, which shot is good to show an actor's facial expressions?

(A) a full shot
(B) a mid-shot
(C) a long shot
(D) a personal shot

9. Which of the following would viewers most likely see in a social shot?

(A) a giant desert of sand
(B) very fine details on an antique lamp
(C) the mouth of a character giving a lecture
(D) the heads and chests of two talking characters

10. According to the passage, which most likely adds intense moments to scary movies?

(A) a long shot
(B) a personal shot
(C) an extreme close-up
(D) an extreme long shot

UNIT 5   Camera Shots

Listening Practice

 Listen and write.

  MP3 J2-5

Camera Shots

Many film viewers know about sound ¹ _____ and ² _____
techniques in movies. But they may not think about the camera shots. A camera shot is
the amount of space that a viewer can see at one time on the screen. There are six main
types of camera shot. An "extreme long shot" shows a movie's ³ _____ . It
is often used at the beginning of the movie to show the main location. A "long shot"
shows a smaller part of the ⁴ _____ of the movie. It may show a building,
for example. A "full shot" shows the characters. In a full shot, viewers can see the actors'
⁵ _____ . This shot helps to show relationships. A "mid-shot" shows people
from the ⁶ _____ to the head. It is also called a "social shot," because it
shows people talking. A "close-up" shows just one character's face. This shot is also
called a "personal shot," because it helps show a character's emotions. An "extreme
close-up" shows just one part of a face or object. Horror movies sometimes use this
technique because it is very intense. These six camera shots help filmmakers tell their
stories.

Word Bank

waste	location	lightning
lighting	costumes	techniques
customs	waist	techniqes
locasion	landscape	landscap

 Listen. Pause. Say each sentence.

  MP3 J2-5G

Writing Practice

 Write the words.

1 _____

n the way that lights are set up

2 _____

n special way to do something

3 _____

n a wide view of a place

4 _____

n a place

5 _____

n the special clothes that an actor wears

6 _____

n the part of the body above the hips and below the chest

 Write the words in each blank.

Summary

There are six _____ types of camera _____: an extreme long shot, a long shot, a _____ shot, a mid-shot, a close-up, and an extreme close-up. These six camera shots help _____ tell their stories.

Word Puzzle

 Complete the word puzzle.

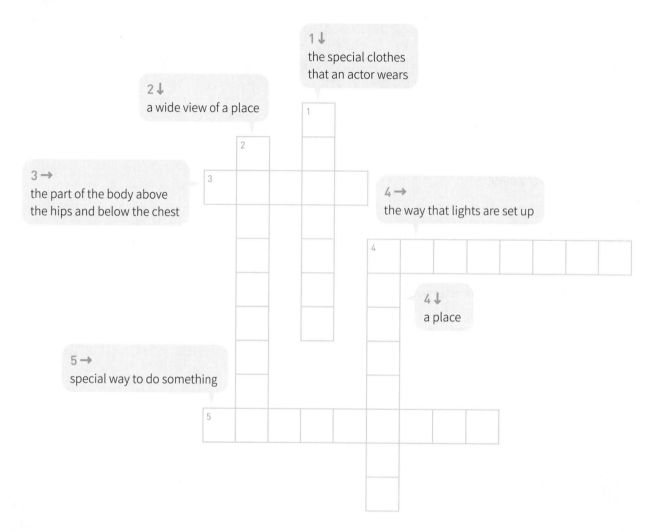

1 ↓
the special clothes that an actor wears

2 ↓
a wide view of a place

3 →
the part of the body above the hips and below the chest

4 →
the way that lights are set up

4 ↓
a place

5 →
special way to do something

UNIT 6

The State Hermitage

Teacher's Book p.130

Name a museum or art gallery in your area.
What kinds of exhibits does it have?

The State Hermitage (or Hermitage) is a museum in Saint Petersburg, Russia. It is one of the world's most famous museums. There are three key reasons it is famous. First, the Hermitage is very big. In fact, it is the second largest art museum in the world. Only the Louvre in Paris is bigger. Secondly, the Hermitage has a great collection of art. It has over three million artworks. It also has important older artworks. When it was built in 1764, the museum held the art collection of the Russian empress Catherine the Great. Catherine enjoyed art and had a lot of money to buy paintings and sculptures. Her art collection even included some paintings by Rembrandt, the famous Dutch painter. Those paintings are still in the museum today. Finally, the Hermitage is famous because its buildings are very beautiful. The museum buildings used to be palaces. The buildings are very fancy, and many rooms are decorated in gold. For these three reasons, visitors from all over go to Saint Petersburg to see the Hermitage.

New Words

collection of	**sculpture**
a group of	*n* a type of work of art
used to be	**fancy**
v was before	*adj* expensive and elegant
decorated	**palace**
adj made to look beautiful	*n* a building where royal or very rich people live

Part A. **Sentence Completion**

1. A: This art museum is so elegant!
    B: Yes, it _____ be a palace.

    (A) uses
    (B) used
    (C) uses to
    (D) used to

2. A: The museum has _____ many artworks to see in a day.
    B: I will just focus on the paintings by Rembrandt.

    (A) as
    (B) too
    (C) little
    (D) very

Part B. **Situational Writing**

3.

    She is working on a new _____.

    (A) novel
    (B) art film
    (C) sculpture
    (D) wood shop

4.

    Look at this incredible _____ books.

    (A) cart of
    (B) box of
    (C) basket of
    (D) collection of

Admission to the State Hermitage Museum

Tickets purchased on the day of your visit:

700 RUB: entry ticket to main museum and its branches

400 RUB: entry ticket to main museum and its branches, entry only for citizens of Russia or Belarus

300 RUB: entry ticket to just one of the museum branches

* 100 RUB = approximately $1.50 US

⭐ **Free entrance:** preschool children, school children, university students with valid ID

⭐ Free entry to all visitors on the first Thursday of each month

5. How much would it cost for 1 school child and 1 adult from Japan to enter the main museum and branches on the Thursday, November 1st?

(A) 500 RUB

(B) 700 RUB

(C) 1400 RUB

(D) nothing

6. Anton is a retired worker from Belarus. What is the minimum price for him to enter one museum branch on weekends?

(A) 100 RUB

(B) 300 RUB

(C) 500 RUB

(D) 700 RUB

Part D. General Reading and Retelling

The State Hermitage (or Hermitage) is a museum in Saint Petersburg, Russia. It is one of the world's most famous museums. There are three key reasons it is famous. First, the Hermitage is very big. In fact, it is the second largest art museum in the world. Only the Louvre in Paris is bigger. Secondly, the Hermitage has a great collection of art. It has over three million artworks. It also has important older artworks. When it was built in 1764, the museum held the art collection of the Russian empress Catherine the Great. Catherine enjoyed art and had a lot of money to buy paintings and sculptures. Her art collection even included some paintings by Rembrandt, the famous Dutch painter. Those paintings are still in the museum today. Finally, the Hermitage is famous because its buildings are very beautiful. The museum buildings used to be palaces. The buildings are very fancy, and many rooms are decorated in gold. For these three reasons, visitors from all over go to Saint Petersburg to see the Hermitage.

7. What is the main idea of the passage?

   (A) The Hermitage is in Saint Petersburg.
   (B) The Hermitage is famous for three reasons.
   (C) The Hermitage has many international visitors.
   (D) The Hermitage has the world's best art collection.

8. According to the passage, what is NOT true about the Hermitage?

   (A) It was built in 1764.
   (B) It holds important old artworks.
   (C) It is bigger than the Louvre in Paris.
   (D) It has over three million works of art.

9. Which artist is mentioned in the passage?

   (A) Picasso
   (B) Matisse
   (C) Vermeer
   (D) Rembrandt

10. According to the passage, what is true about the Hermitage buildings?

   (A) They burned down twice.
   (B) They used to be palaces.
   (C) They have sixty bathrooms.
   (D) They are made from gold bricks.

Listening Practice

 Listen and write.

  MP3 J2-6

The State Hermitage

The State Hermitage (or Hermitage) is a museum in Saint Petersburg, Russia. It is one of the world's most famous museums. There are three key reasons it is famous. First, the Hermitage is very big. In fact, it is the second largest art museum in the world. Only the Louvre in Paris is bigger. Secondly, the Hermitage has a great

1 _____ of art. It has over three million artworks. It also has important older artworks. When it was built in 1764, the museum held the art collection of the Russian empress Catherine the Great. Catherine enjoyed art and had a lot of money to buy paintings and 2 _____. Her art collection even included some paintings by Rembrandt, the famous Dutch painter. Those paintings are still in the museum today. Finally, the Hermitage is famous because its buildings are very beautiful. The museum buildings 3 _____ to be 4 _____. The buildings are very 5 _____, and many rooms are 6 _____ in gold. For these three reasons, visitors from all over go to Saint Petersburg to see the Hermitage.

Word Bank

palaces	scuptures	fency
colection	use	sculptures
used	decorate	pallaces
fancy	decorated	collection

 Listen. Pause. Say each sentence.

  MP3 J2-6G

Writing Practice

 Write the words.

1 _____ a group of	2 _____ *n* a type of work of art
3 _____ *v* was before	4 _____ *adj* expensive and elegant
5 _____ *adj* made to look beautiful	6 _____ *n* a building where royal or very rich people live

 Write the words in each blank.

Summary

The State Hermitage is one of the world's most famous _____. It is famous for its size, its great collection, and its beautiful _____. It holds over three _____ artworks. Visitors from all over the _____ go to the Hermitage.

Word Puzzle

  Complete the word puzzle.

1 ↓
a building where royal or very rich people live

2 →
expensive and elegant

5 ↓
made to look beautiful

3 ↓
a type of work of art

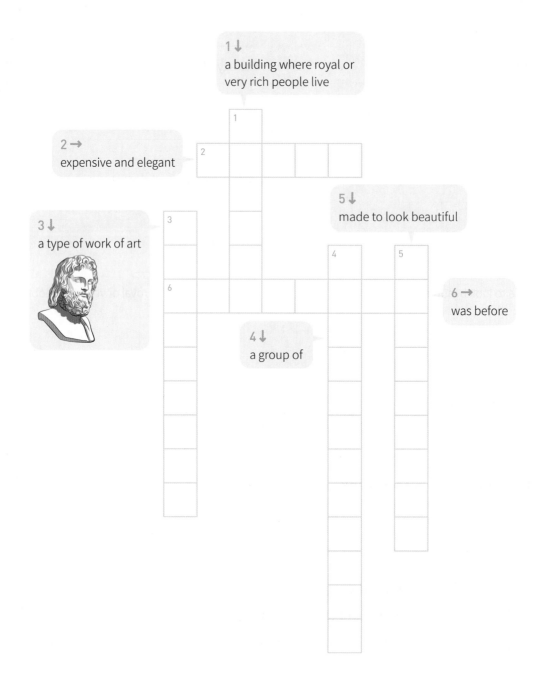

6 →
was before

4 ↓
a group of

Teacher's Book
p.135

UNIT 7

Persian Miniatures

Can you guess where and
when this kind of artwork was created?

UNIT 7 Persian Miniatures

Persian miniatures are very detailed, small paintings made in the part of the Middle East that is now Iran. Although modern artists are still painting Persian miniatures today, this form of art was most popular between the 13th to the 16th centuries. Persian miniatures often appeared in beautifully created religious or traditional books. Making them required careful hands and a fine paint brush. Because each miniature could take more than a year to complete, only very wealthy people could afford to get one. Even viewing a miniature takes time. Persian miniatures feature extremely complex scenes. They have a kind of layered effect that is similar to a 3D perspective. Therefore, viewers need time to appreciate everything in the painting, from the stunning, bright colors to the parts of the painting made of real gold and silver. Observers should also note the interesting geometric patterns in each Persian miniature. It is a mystery how an artist could get so much detail into works of art as tiny as a Persian miniature.

New Words

wealthy

adj rich

fine

adj very thin

afford to do X

v have enough money to do X

feature

v have and show

perspective

n point of view

tiny

adj extremely small

Part A. Sentence Completion

1. A: Look at these tiny artworks!
    B: Aren't they beautiful? _____ one has a special theme.

    (A) All
    (B) Both
    (C) Each
    (D) Many

2. A: How did they make such tiny artworks?
    B: They _____ used extremely small brushes, I guess.

    (A) must be
    (B) should be
    (C) must have
    (D) should have

Part B. Situational Writing

3.

For these details, you need a really _____ brush. Use the purple one.

(A) tall
(B) fine
(C) thick
(D) fan-shaped

4.

He sold his art, and now he is quite _____.

(A) upset
(B) sporty
(C) wealthy
(D) disappointed

Course: Make a Persian Miniature Painting

In this class, you will learn how to appreciate, draw, and paint flowers using traditional Persian miniature techniques. In addition, students will learn how to prepare the special paper and paint you need.

What to bring:

Brushes: Jilali brand brushes in sizes 1.1, 2, and 2.1
Click here to see examples.
We will provide all other required materials.

This course is for: painters of all levels and ages

Course days: Mondays / Wednesdays: 9:00-noon

5. According to the ad, what will students learn?

(A) how to draw flowers
(B) how to buy paintings
(C) how to paint animals
(D) how to appreciate vases

6. What is true about the class?

(A) The course is just for preschoolers.
(B) It takes place on Monday afternoons.
(C) Participants should have their own paint.
(D) Students should bring particular brushes.

Part D. General Reading and Retelling

Persian miniatures are very detailed, small paintings made in the part of the Middle East that is now Iran. Although modern artists are still painting Persian miniatures today, this form of art was most popular between the 13th to the 16th centuries. Persian miniatures often appeared in beautifully created religious or traditional books. Making them required careful hands and a fine paint brush. Because each miniature could take more than a year to complete, only very wealthy people could afford to get one. Even viewing a miniature takes time. Persian miniatures feature extremely complex scenes. They have a kind of layered effect that is similar to a 3D perspective. Therefore, viewers need time to appreciate everything in the painting, from the stunning, bright colors to the parts of the painting made of real gold and silver. Observers should also note the interesting geometric patterns in each Persian miniature. It is a mystery how an artist could get so much detail into works of art as tiny as a Persian miniature.

7. Which is the best title for the passage?

(A) Persia: Its Ancient Gardens
(B) Persian Miniatures: Small Horses
(C) Persian Miniatures: Tiny Paintings
(D) Persia: The History of the Middle East

8. According to the passage, in which century were Persian miniatures likely most popular?

(A) 12th
(B) 14th
(C) 17th
(D) 20th

9. According to the passage, what is true about Persian miniatures in the past?

(A) They each took a month to complete.
(B) They were banned in religious books.
(C) Only really rich people could get them.
(D) They were painted in black, white, and gray.

10. According to the passage, what is most likely needed now to appreciate a Persian miniature?

(A) silver coins
(B) enough time
(C) bright clothing
(D) math knowledge

Listening Practice

 Listen and write.

  MP3 J2-7

Persian Miniatures

Persian miniatures are very detailed, small paintings made in the part of the Middle East that is now Iran. Although modern artists are still painting Persian miniatures today, this form of art was most popular between the 13th to the 16th centuries. Persian miniatures often appeared in beautifully created religious or traditional books. Making them required careful hands and a ¹ _____ paint brush. Because each miniature could take more than a year to complete, only very ² _____ people could ³ _____ to get one. Even viewing a miniature takes time. Persian miniatures ⁴ _____ extremely complex scenes. They have a kind of layered effect that is similar to a 3D ⁵ _____. Therefore, viewers need time to appreciate everything in the painting, from the stunning, bright colors to the parts of the painting made of real gold and silver. Observers should also note the interesting geometric patterns in each Persian miniature. It is a mystery how an artist could get so much detail into works of art as ⁶ _____ as a Persian miniature.

Word Bank

fine	feature	tinny
aford	find	welthy
wealthy	afford	tiny
perspective	ferspective	fiture

 Listen. Pause. Say each sentence.

  MP3 J2-7G

Writing Practice

Write the words.

1 _____

adj rich

2 _____

adj very thin

3 _____ X

v have enough money to do X

4 _____

v have and show

5 _____

n point of view

6 _____

adj extremely small

Write the words in each blank.

Summary

Persian miniatures are very detailed, small _____ made in the _____ East. Each miniature takes a lot of _____ to make and view _____ its extremely complex scenes.

Word Puzzle

Complete the word puzzle.

1 ↓ point of view

3 ↓ extremely small

2 → rich

4 ↓ have enough money to do X

5 → have and show

6 → very thin

Teacher's Book
p.140

UNIT 8

Animals Symbols

Think about art in your culture.
Which animals are common symbols in art?

UNIT 8 Animals Symbols

Koreans have long used important mammals, birds, and reptiles as symbols in art. Probably one of the most common animal symbols in Korea is the tiger. It appears on clothing and as mascots at sporting events. To Koreans, tigers represent courage and strength. Another animal symbol, the white crane, stands for long life. Cranes often appear with pine trees in architecture, on holiday cards, and on jewelry boxes. Long life is also represented by the turtle. Some Koreans believed that turtles could tell the future. Turtle images now form the base of many famous monuments. Finally, ducks in art show a happy marriage bond. Duck couples in nature stay together their whole lives, so many Korean couples receive wooden ducks when they get married. With these animal symbols, Korean society has represented important ideas about life through art.

New Words

mammal

n an animal with warm blood and fur

reptile

n an animal with cold blood and dry skin

mascot

n a symbol for a group

crane

n a white bird with a long neck

stand for

v mean

monument

n an important statue or building

Part A. Sentence Completion

1. A: What is a popular animal symbol in Africa?
   B: One of the most popular symbols _____ the zebra.

   (A) is
   (B) do
   (C) are
   (D) does

2. A: Ducks represent a happy marriage in Korea.
   B: So that's _____ wooden ducks are a wedding gift there!

   (A) it
   (B) why
   (C) when
   (D) because

Part B. Situational Writing

3.

This card shows three white _____.

   (A) clouds
   (B) planes
   (C) cranes
   (D) peacocks

4.

Jen likes learning about _____.

   (A) birds
   (B) insects
   (C) reptiles
   (D) mammals

Animal Symbols in Renaissance Art

Animals	Symbolized:
Dogs	loyalty / serving a master / being rich
Monkeys	humans / art skills: painting and sculpture
Peacocks	pride / living forever
Parrots	speaking fluently / being rich
Snakes	medicine / lying
Lions	power (especially as a king)

5. What did peacocks represent?

   (A) wealth
   (B) beauty
   (C) never dying
   (D) always dancing

6. Which animal symbol is related to helping humans?

   (A) lions
   (B) dogs
   (C) parrots
   (D) monkeys

Koreans have long used important mammals, birds, and reptiles as symbols in art. Probably one of the most common animal symbols in Korea is the tiger. It appears on clothing and as mascots at sporting events. To Koreans, tigers represent courage and strength. Another animal symbol, the white crane, stands for long life. Cranes often appear with pine trees in architecture, on holiday cards, and on jewelry boxes. Long life is also represented by the turtle. Some Koreans believed that turtles could tell the future. Turtle images now form the base of many famous monuments. Finally, ducks in art show a happy marriage bond. Duck couples in nature stay together their whole lives, so many Korean couples receive wooden ducks when they get married. With these animal symbols, Korean society has represented important ideas about life through art.

7. What is the main idea of the passage?

   (A) Korea has many folk tales about animals.
   (B) Korean cooking has developed over time.
   (C) Korea has fewer animals now than in the past.
   (D) Korean culture uses animals to teach life lessons.

8. On which blog would this passage most likely be found?

   (A) Art of Korea
   (B) Asian Comedy
   (C) Alleys in Seoul
   (D) Animals in Danger

9. Which animal is mentioned in the passage?

   (A) the frog
   (B) the deer
   (C) the turtle
   (D) the rabbit

10. What does the passage mention about cranes?

   (A) They are often painted with clouds.
   (B) They sometimes appear on clothing.
   (C) They are often shown on jewelry boxes.
   (D) They sometimes symbolize lonely people.

Listening Practice

 Listen and write.

  MP3 J2-8

Animals Symbols

Koreans have long used important ¹ _____ , birds, and ² _____ as symbols in art. Probably one of the most common animal symbols in Korea is the tiger. It appears on clothing and as ³ _____ at sporting events. To Koreans, tigers represent courage and strength. Another animal symbol, the white crane, ⁴ _____ long life. ⁵ _____ often appear with pine trees in architecture, on holiday cards, and on jewelry boxes. Long life is also represented by the turtle. Some Koreans believed that turtles could tell the future. Turtle images now form the base of many famous ⁶ _____ . Finally, ducks in art show a happy marriage bond. Duck couples in nature stay together their whole lives, so many Korean couples receive wooden ducks when they get married. With these animal symbols, Korean society has represented important ideas about life through art.

Word Bank

retpiles	reptiles	mamals
monuments	stands for	cranes
monumants	Cranes	mescots
standsfor	mammals	mascots

 Listen. Pause. Say each sentence.

  MP3 J2-8G

Writing Practice

 Write the words.

1 _____

   n an animal with warm blood and fur

2 _____

   n an animal with cold blood and dry skin

3 _____

   n a symbol for a group

4 _____

   n a white bird with a long neck

5 _____

   v mean

6 _____

   n an important statue or building

 Write the words in each blank.

Summary

Koreans have long used important animals as _____ in art. These include tigers, _____, and ducks. With these animal symbols, _____ society has expressed important ideas about _____ through art.

Word Puzzle

 Complete the word puzzle.

1 ↓
a symbol for a group

2 ↓
an important statue
or building

3 →
mean

4 ↓
an animal with
warm blood and fur

5 →
a white bird
with a long
neck

6 →
an animal with cold
blood and dry skin

The Mysteries of *Salvator Mundi* ——

Teacher's Book
p.145

In 2017, a painting called *Salvator Mundi*, an artwork from the year 1500, was sold at a famous auction house. The selling price was an incredible $450,000,000. That made it the most expensive artwork ever sold. The reason the painting was worth so much money is because the artist was supposed to be Leonardo da Vinci, the same artist who painted the *Mona Lisa*. However, some art historians believe that da Vinci painted only about one fifth of the painting. The rest of the painting was done by da Vinci's assistant, Bernardino Luini. Of course, other art experts disagree, and it is not really known how much of the painting was done by the master, da Vinci, and how much was done by his student.

Adding to the mystery of *Salvator Mundi* is its present location. The painting was bought by a Saudi prince. However, the prince had not displayed the painting in a museum. It is not certain if the painting is in his home. At one point, the painting may even have been on the prince's boat, but this is also not certain. The only certain thing is that *Salvator Mundi* is both very valuable and incredibly mysterious.

CHAPTER 3

Music

UNIT 9

Musical vs. Opera

Musical

Opera

Would you rather watch a musical or an opera? Why?

Musicals and opera both involve a live performance of a story that includes songs. So what is the difference between the two art forms? Some people claim that musicals are more showy. They include elements like tap dance and comedy. Opera, meanwhile, may seem more serious. However, this distinction is not always true. Some musicals, such as "Les Miserables," are more dramatic than humorous. Other people think that opera involves pure singing, whereas musicals involve both spoken words and singing. But actually in some musicals, the performers also sing the whole time. It may seem, therefore, that there are no clear lines dividing musicals from opera. However, one expert has pointed out a key difference: the lyrics. He says that in opera, music is the most important part, while in musicals, it is the words that are more important. Opera has lyrics, of course, but the stories are more general. Moreover, the details of the lyrics are not as important. In musicals, clever lyrics give the story its special meaning. The difference may not always be clear, but perhaps there is a small distinction between musicals and operas after all.

New Words

claim	spoken
v argue	*adj* said with words out loud

key	lyrics
adj important	*n* the words of a song

clever	distinction
adj smart	*n* difference

Part A. Sentence Completion

1. A: What is the difference _____ rap music and hip-hop?

    B: Actually, the difference is not always clear.

    (A) in

    (B) of

    (C) from

    (D) between

2. A: Which do you prefer: opera or musicals?

    B: I think opera is so-so, _____ I really love musicals.

    (A) or

    (B) so

    (C) but

    (D) then

Part B. Situational Writing

3.

The kids know all the _____.

(A) lyrics

(B) novels

(C) paintings

(D) sculptures

4.

The _____ fox will get the cheese.

(A) black

(B) flying

(C) clever

(D) sleeping

UNIT 9   Musical vs. Opera

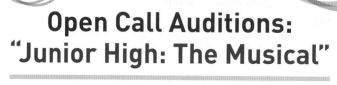

Open Call Auditions: "Junior High: The Musical"

Can you sing, dance, and act?
Then why not audition for "Junior High: The Musical"?
This musical includes both traditional Broadway-style song-and-dance numbers as well as some opera songs.
We need people who can:

   1) sing an operatic aria   2) tap dance and do the waltz

Saturday March 16th: 9:00 AM to 1:00 PM
Kendrick Middle School Theater

We also need backstage volunteers:
costume designers, set designers, and builders.

For more information, email Kathy at kathymusical@internet.com

5.   What is true about the auditions?

   (A) They will be held in a gym.

   (B) They take place on a Sunday.

   (C) They occur over a four-hour period.

   (D) They are for a classical opera performance.

6.   According to the advertisement, who among the following would most likely be needed?

   (A) someone who can film actors

   (B) someone who can dance ballet

   (C) someone who knows the best camera shots

   (D) someone who knows how to construct a set

Musicals and opera both involve a live performance of a story that includes songs. So what is the difference between the two art forms? Some people claim that musicals are more showy. They include elements like tap dance and comedy. Opera, meanwhile, may seem more serious. However, this distinction is not always true. Some musicals, such as "Les Miserables," are more dramatic than humorous. Other people think that opera involves pure singing, whereas musicals involve both spoken words and singing. But actually in some musicals, the performers also sing the whole time. It may seem, therefore, that there are no clear lines dividing musicals from opera. However, one expert has pointed out a key difference: the lyrics. He says that in opera, music is the most important part, while in musicals, it is the words that are more important. Opera has lyrics, of course, but the stories are more general. Moreover, the details of the lyrics are not as important. In musicals, clever lyrics give the story its special meaning. The difference may not always be clear, but perhaps there is a small distinction between musicals and operas after all.

7. What is the passage mainly about?

    (A) the costumes in musicals and opera
    (B) how musicals became more operatic
    (C) the difference between musicals and opera
    (D) why musicals are more popular than opera

8. Which aspect of musicals and operas is mentioned?

    (A) seating
    (B) lighting
    (C) directors
    (D) performers

9. What statement does the passage say is not always true?

    (A) Opera performers hate tap dancing.
    (B) Opera is more serious than musicals.
    (C) Opera performers have a lot of training.
    (D) Opera is more expensive than musicals.

10. According to the passage, what has one expert said about musicals and opera?

    (A) The stories in opera are silly.
    (B) In opera, people sometimes speak a lot.
    (C) The dancing in musicals makes them special.
    (D) In musicals, words are more important than the music.

UNIT 9   Musical vs. Opera

Listening Practice

 Listen and write.

  MP3 J2-9

Musical vs. Opera

Musicals and opera both involve a live performance of a story that includes songs. So what is the difference between the two art forms? Some people ¹ _____ that musicals are more showy. They include elements like tap dance and comedy. Opera, meanwhile, may seem more serious. However, this distinction is not always true. Some musicals, such as "Les Miserables," are more dramatic than humorous. Other people think that opera involves pure singing, whereas musicals involve both ² _____ words and singing. But actually in some musicals, the performers also sing the whole time. It may seem, therefore, that there are no clear lines dividing musicals from opera. However, one expert has pointed out a ³ _____ difference: the ⁴ _____ . He says that in opera, music is the most important part, while in musicals, it is the words that are more important. Opera has lyrics, of course, but the stories are more general. Moreover, the details of the lyrics are not as important. In musicals, ⁵ _____ lyrics give the story its special meaning. The difference may not always be clear, but perhaps there is a small ⁶ _____ between musicals and operas after all.

Word Bank

Lyrics	keys	clever
key	clame	distinction
spocken	clevel	spoken
claim	lyrics	distenction

 Listen. Pause. Say each sentence.

  MP3 J2-9G

Writing Practice

 Write the words.

1 _____

   v   argue

2 _____

   adj   said with words out loud

3 _____

   adj   important

4 _____

   n   the words of a song

5 _____

   adj   smart

6 _____

   n   difference

 Write the words in each blank.

Summary

The distinction between musicals and _____ is not always clear. However,

a key difference _____ musicals and opera may be the _____ .

In opera, maybe _____ is the most important part, while in musicals, the

words matter more.

Word Puzzle

Complete the word puzzle.

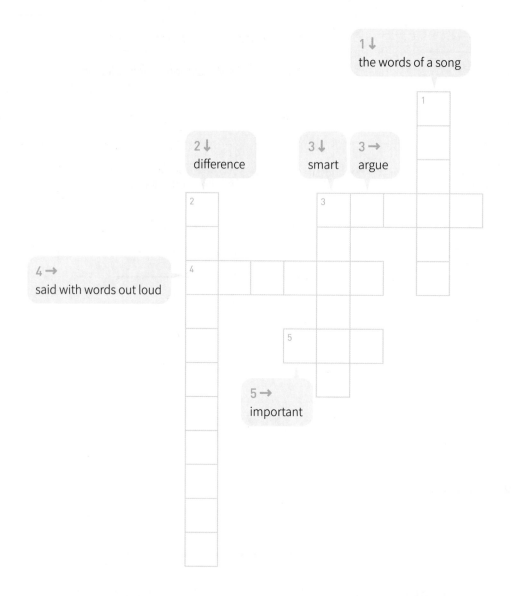

1 ↓
the words of a song

2 ↓
difference

3 ↓
smart

3 →
argue

4 →
said with words out loud

5 →
important

Teacher's Book
p.151

UNIT 10

Vivaldi's "The Four Seasons"

Antonio Vivaldi

Ludwig van Beethoven

Wolfgang
Amadeus Mozart

Frederic Chopin

Do you listen to classical music?
How many composers can you name?

UNIT 10 Vivaldi's "The Four Seasons"

These days, Vivaldi's classical piece "The Four Seasons" will sound very familiar to many people's ears. However, when Italian audiences first heard this piece in 1725, it was completely new. What Vivaldi had done was something called "program music." Program music is when a composer puts writing, like a poem, into musical form. One day, Vivaldi saw some beautiful paintings. Then, he found or wrote some poems on the themes from the paintings. After that, he took the themes from the poems and put them into song. "The Four Seasons" is not the first example of program music. But before Vivaldi wrote it, program music was not considered high art. Even after "The Four Seasons," program music did not become popular until many years later. So when a symphony played the beautiful sounds of "The Four Seasons" to an Italian audience, people were shocked and delighted. Music lovers enjoyed hearing a barking dog, chirping birds, and crackling fire in song form. Today, people have listened to "The Four Seasons" so often that it now represents classical music.

New Words

classical

adj traditional

composer

n a person who write songs

theme

n a topic

audience

n a group of people at a concert

shocked

adj extremely surprised

delighted

adj happy

Part A. Sentence Completion

1. A: What's the name of this song? It sounds very _____.
    B: It's a hip-hop version of a classical song.

    (A) familiar
    (B) familiarly
    (C) familiarity
    (D) more familiar

2. A: Have you heard this song before?
    B: Oh yes. I've listened to it _____ I know all the lyrics.

    (A) often
    (B) as often
    (C) it is often
    (D) so often that

Part B. Situational Writing

3.

    There were at least a hundred people _____.

    (A) on the roof
    (B) in the band
    (C) on the stage
    (D) in the audience

4.

    He is a _____.

    (A) chef
    (B) novelist
    (C) architect
    (D) composer

Concert Reviews

Reviewer 1

How special it was to see "The Four Seasons" performed when we were in Venice. Everyone who visits Venice must do this! The music and church setting are breathtaking.

Reviewer 2

Hearing the crisp, beautiful tones of Vivaldi's music in a church in Venice was the highlight of our trip to Italy.

Reviewer 3

This is an incredible concert. They played the music on vintage instruments from a museum!

Reviewer 4

The musicians really interpret the music so vividly. You can hear thunder, bird calls, and spring rain. The all-age audience loved it. Incredible!

5. Which of the following is true?

    (A) Reviewer 1 thinks the show is a tourist must-see in Venice.
    (B) Reviewer 2 likes that the show took place in a Greek temple.
    (C) Reviewer 3 believes the event place should be bigger.
    (D) Reviewer 4 missed half of the whole show because of rain.

6. According to the reviews, what is most likely true about the concert?

    (A) It took place in a church.
    (B) Vivaldi attended the concert.
    (C) Musicians were on gondola boats.
    (D) Children were not allowed to attend.

These days, Vivaldi's classical piece "The Four Seasons" will sound very familiar to many people's ears. However, when Italian audiences first heard this piece in 1725, it was completely new. What Vivaldi had done was something called "program music." Program music is when a composer puts writing, like a poem, into musical form. One day, Vivaldi saw some beautiful paintings. Then, he found or wrote some poems on the themes from the paintings. After that, he took the themes from the poems and put them into song. "The Four Seasons" is not the first example of program music. But before Vivaldi wrote it, program music was not considered high art. Even after "The Four Seasons," program music did not become popular until many years later. So when a symphony played the beautiful sounds of "The Four Seasons" to an Italian audience, people were shocked and delighted. Music lovers enjoyed hearing a barking dog, chirping birds, and crackling fire in song form. Today, people have listened to "The Four Seasons" so often that it now represents classical music.

7. Which of the following is the best title for the passage?

(A) Italy's First Classical Song
(B) Vivaldi's Special Classical Piece
(C) Computers That Program Music
(D) Regions That Have Four Seasons

8. According to the passage, what is program music?

(A) when poets learn to play the piano
(B) when singers perform music in films
(C) when composers turn writing into song
(D) when writers listen to music while walking

9. According to the passage, what is true about "The Four Seasons"?

(A) Italian royalty banned it from theatres.
(B) Italians hearing it in 1725 were shocked.
(C) It instantly made program music popular.
(D) It was the first example of program music.

10. According to the passage, which is represented in "The Four Seasons"?

(A) a crying baby
(B) a barking dog
(C) a meowing cat
(D) a whistling train

Listening Practice

 Listen and write.

  MP3 J2-10

Vivaldi's "The Four Seasons"

These days, Vivaldi's ¹ _____ piece "The Four Seasons" will sound very familiar to many people's ears. However, when Italian audiences first heard this piece in 1725, it was completely new. What Vivaldi had done was something called "program music." Program music is when a ² _____ puts writing, like a poem, into musical form. One day, Vivaldi saw some beautiful paintings. Then, he found or wrote some poems on the themes from the paintings. After that, he took the ³ _____ from the poems and put them into song. "The Four Seasons" is not the first example of program music. But before Vivaldi wrote it, program music was not considered high art. Even after "The Four Seasons," program music did not become popular until many years later. So when a symphony played the beautiful sounds of "The Four Seasons" to an Italian ⁴ _____, people were ⁵ _____ and ⁶ _____. Music lovers enjoyed hearing a barking dog, chirping birds, and crackling fire in song form. Today, people have listened to "The Four Seasons" so often that it now represents classical music.

Word Bank

shoked	audiance	clasical
compozer	audience	themes
temes	delited	shocked
delighted	classical	composer

 Listen. Pause. Say each sentence.

  MP3 J2-10G

Writing Practice

 Write the words.

1 _____

adj traditional

2 _____

n a person who write songs

3 _____

n a topic

4 _____

n a group of people at a concert

5 _____

adj extremely surprised

6 _____

adj happy

 Write the words in each blank.

Summary

Vivaldi's "The Four Seasons" was completely new when it was first released. Vivaldi turned some _____ into song, and people were _____ and delighted when they heard this song. Today, "The Four _____" is so popular that it represents _____ music.

Word Puzzle

 Complete the word puzzle.

1 → a person who write songs

2 ↓ extremely surprised

3 ↓ traditional

4 ↓ a topic

5 ↓ happy

6 → a group of people at a concert

UNIT 11

Dynamics in Music

Teacher's Book
p.156

Do you recognize any of symbols in the image?
What do you think they are?

People who read and play music have to understand a little Italian. Italian words and symbols are used to show how loudly music should be played. The music word 'piano' means 'quietly' or 'softly,' and 'forte' means 'loudly.' In written music, 'piano' becomes 'p' and forte becomes 'f.' In addition, 'mezzo' means 'moderately,' and becomes 'm.' Also, when music words end with '-issimo,' it means 'very' and it can become 'pp' or 'ff.' This gives us six key ways to show the volume of music. First, 'ff' is 'fortissimo' and means 'very loudly.' An 'f' is 'forte' and means 'loudly' while 'mf' is 'mezzo forte' and means 'moderately loudly.' In addition, 'mp' is 'mezzo piano' and means 'moderately quietly.' A 'p' means 'piano' or 'quietly,' and 'pp' is 'pianissimo' and means 'very quietly.' These words are very important to music. Interestingly, the instruments we now call pianos were first called a 'pianofortes' because they could be played both loudly and quietly. These days we only use the first part of the full word.

New Words

symbol

n a sign that represents something else

in addition

adv also

moderately

adv a bit, but not too strongly

end with

v have in their last part

volume

n the loudness or quietness of a sound

interestingly

adv it is interesting that

Part A. Sentence Completion

1. A: What _____ this word mean? I don't speak Italian.
    B: It means "quietly."

    (A) is
    (B) do
    (C) are
    (D) does

2. A: What are all these symbols?
    B: They're music words. They show _____ loudly we should play music.

    (A) too
    (B) very
    (C) how
    (D) which

Part B. Situational Writing

3.

These buttons control the _____ on my computer.

(A) color
(B) picture
(C) volume
(D) download

4.

On this happiness scale, yellow means you are _____ happy.

(A) not at all
(B) moderately
(C) always
(D) very

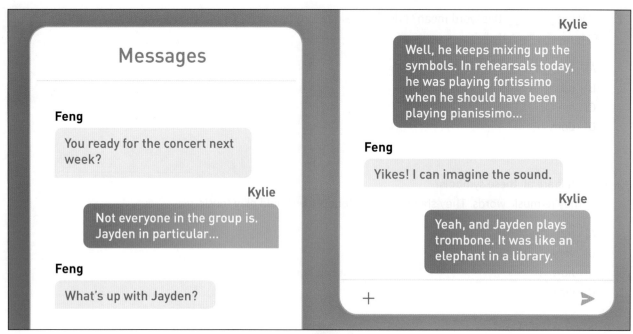

5. What is Kylie's problem?

    (A) She was yelled at by Jayden.
    (B) She cannot easily read music.
    (C) She forgot the words to a song.
    (D) She thinks Jayden is not prepared.

6. What is probably meant by, "It was like an elephant in a library"?

    (A) There was a big person in a small room.
    (B) There was a loud sound in a quiet place.
    (C) There was an old instrument in a new area.
    (D) There was an interesting animal in a boring building.

People who read and play music have to understand a little Italian. Italian words and symbols are used to show how loudly music should be played. The music word 'piano' means 'quietly' or 'softly,' and 'forte' means 'loudly.' In written music, 'piano' becomes 'p' and forte becomes 'f.' In addition, 'mezzo' means 'moderately,' and becomes 'm.' Also, when music words end with '-issimo,' it means 'very' and it can become 'pp' or 'ff.' This gives us six key ways to show the volume of music. First, 'ff' is 'fortissimo' and means 'very loudly.' An 'f' is 'forte' and means 'loudly' while 'mf' is 'mezzo forte' and means 'moderately loudly.' In addition, 'mp' is 'mezzo piano' and means 'moderately quietly.' A 'p' means 'piano' or 'quietly,' and 'pp' is 'pianissimo' and means 'very quietly.' These words are very important to music. Interestingly, the instruments we now call pianos were first called a 'pianofortes' because they could be played both loudly and quietly. These days we only use the first part of the full word.

7. What is the passage mainly about?

   (A) how instruments got their names
   (B) Italian words and symbols in music
   (C) why students should learn two languages
   (D) how modern music is worse than classical music

8. According to the passage, which music word means "moderately"?

   (A) mixto
   (B) mezzo
   (C) mestizo
   (D) mozzarella

9. According to the passage, how many ways are there to show volume?

   (A) six
   (B) seven
   (C) eight
   (D) nine

10. According to the passage, why did pianofortes get that name?

   (A) because they had strong legs
   (B) because they were both quiet and loud
   (C) because they were made from unique wood
   (D) because they had both black and white keys

Listening Practice

 Listen and write.

  MP3 J2-11

Dynamics in Music

People who read and play music have to understand a little Italian. Italian words and

¹ _____ are used to show how loudly music should be played. The music word 'piano' means 'quietly' or 'softly,' and 'forte' means 'loudly.' In written music, 'piano' becomes 'p' and forte becomes 'f.' In addition, 'mezzo' means 'moderately,' and becomes 'm.' Also, when music words ² _____ with '-issimo,' it means 'very' and it can become 'pp' or 'ff.' This gives us six key ways to show the ³ _____ of music. First, 'ff' is 'fortissimo' and means 'very loudly.' An 'f' is 'forte' and means 'loudly' while 'mf' is 'mezzo forte' and means 'moderately loudly.' ⁴ _____ , 'mp' is 'mezzo piano' and means ' ⁵ _____ quietly.' A 'p' means 'piano' or 'quietly,' and 'pp' is 'pianissimo' and means 'very quietly.' These words are very important to music. ⁶ _____ , the instruments we now call pianos were first called a 'pianofortes' because they could be played both loudly and quietly. These days we only use the first part of the full word.

Word Bank

volume	symbals	end
In addition	symbols	moderatly
and	bolume	moderately
In adition	Interestingly	Intrestingly

 Listen. Pause. Say each sentence.

  MP3 J2-11G

Writing Practice

Write the words.

1 _____

n a sign that represents something else

2 _____

adv also

3 _____

adv a bit, but not too strongly

4 _____

v have in their last part

5 _____

n the loudness or quietness of a sound

6 _____

adv it is interesting that

 Write the words in each blank.

Summary

Italian words are used to show the _____ of music. "Piano" means

"_____," "forte" means "_____," and "mezzo" means

"_____." When music words end with "-issimo," it means "very."

Word Puzzle

  Complete the word puzzle.

1 ↓
it is interesting that

2 ↓
the loudness or quietness of a sound

3 ↓
a bit, but not too strongly

4 →
a sign that represents something else

5 →
have in their last part

6 →
also

Teacher's Book
p.161

UNIT 12

The Alphorn

Do you know the name of the instrument in the picture?
What kind of sound might it make?

The alphorn is Europe's antique cellphone. The long cone shape of the instrument allows it to be heard far away. It is very effective in areas with natural echoes, such as mountains and valleys. For many years, it was used to communicate in the mountains of Switzerland, Austria, Germany, and Northern Italy. In the 17th to 19th centuries, alphorns were used as signals in village communities there. They were often used when there were no church bells. However, they were mostly used by people who kept cattle herds. The horns let them communicate with other cow owners in the neighboring mountains. They could even signal people in the nearest village. Moreover, they could call the cows from the fields to the dairy when it was milking time. Alphorn music was then used to relax the cows while they were being milked. Today, alphorns are still used in festivals, TV commercials, and as tourist attractions. Sadly, the fascinating signal function of the alphorn and its uses to call or calm cattle have been lost.

New Words

effective

adj powerful

cattle

n cows

herd

n a group of animals such as cows or deer

communicate with

v have contact with

signal

n an action or sound to get someone's attention

dairy

n a farm where milk and cheese are made

Part A. Sentence Completion

1. A: What's that?
    B: It's a typewriter. Before computers, people used these _____ write letters.

    (A) if
    (B) to
    (C) for
    (D) when

2. A: Do people still play these instruments?
    B: Sure. They're used in special events, _____ festivals.

    (A) so as
    (B) as so
    (C) such as
    (D) as such

Part B. Situational Writing

3.

    Year: 1789

    You must not sit in that _____ chair.

    (A) violet
    (B) metal
    (C) rocking
    (D) antique

4.

    She keeps _____.

    (A) cattle
    (B) geese
    (C) rabbits
    (D) turkeys

Hi Jaehyung,

How's life in Mokpo? Here in Spiez, life is great. Guess what! We learned to play the alphorn at school today. You may think it's easy to play. Trust me- it's not! The alphorn is 3 meters long, so it's really hard to make a sound. Not only that, but you have to control every note with your breath. Basically, we stood in the grass on the side of a mountain and spit into an alphorn. Some cows watched us. I've attached a picture of our teacher!

Anyway, I'm having lots of fun here.
Can't wait to hear your news!

Missing you,
Marco

5.   Who is in the photo?

(A)   Marco
(B)   Jaehyung
(C)   Marco's teacher
(D)   Jaehyung's teacher

6.   What does Marco say about playing the alphorn?

(A)   It was easier than he expected.
(B)   The lesson was observed by cows.
(C)   It required complicated finger moves.
(D)   The instrument was almost 2 meters long.

The alphorn is Europe's antique cellphone. The long cone shape of the instrument allows it to be heard far away. It is very effective in areas with natural echoes, such as mountains and valleys. For many years, it was used to communicate in the mountains of Switzerland, Austria, Germany, and Northern Italy. In the 17th to 19th centuries, alphorns were used as signals in village communities there. They were often used when there were no church bells. However, they were mostly used by people who kept cattle herds. The horns let them communicate with other cow owners in the neighboring mountains. They could even signal people in the nearest village. Moreover, they could call the cows from the fields to the dairy when it was milking time. Alphorn music was then used to relax the cows while they were being milked. Today, alphorns are still used in festivals, TV commercials, and as tourist attractions. Sadly, the fascinating signal function of the alphorn and its uses to call or calm cattle have been lost.

7. Which of the following would be the best title for the passage?

(A) How to Play an Alphorn
(B) Where to Buy an Alphorn
(C) Why Cows Like Alphorns
(D) How Alphorns Were Used

8. According to the passage, where would an alphorn most likely have been used in the 18th century?

(A) at a farm in Peru
(B) in a Chinese dairy
(C) on a Swiss mountain
(D) near a Japanese volcano

9. Which use of alphorns is NOT mentioned?

(A) to calm milk cows
(B) to stop animal thieves
(C) to replace church bells
(D) to get cows out of a field

10. Which of these statements would the writer most likely agree with?

(A) "People playing alphorns looked silly."
(B) "Cows should learn to play the alphorn."
(C) "The signal function of alphorns was interesting."
(D) "The main purpose of alphorns was to show off wealth."

UNIT 12　The Alphorn

Listen and write.

  MP3 J2-12

The Alphorn

The alphorn is Europe's antique cellphone. The long cone shape of the instrument allows it to be heard far away. It is very ¹ _____ in areas with natural echoes, such as mountains and valleys. For many years, it was used to communicate in the mountains of Switzerland, Austria, Germany, and Northern Italy. In the 17th to 19th centuries, alphorns were used as signals in village communities there. They were often used when there were no church bells. However, they were mostly used by people who kept cattle ² _____. The horns let them ³ _____ with other cow owners in the neighboring mountains. They could even signal people in the nearest village. Moreover, they could call the cows from the fields to the ⁴ _____ when it was milking time. Alphorn music was then used to relax the cows while they were being milked. Today, alphorns are still used in festivals, TV commercials, and as tourist attractions. Sadly, the fascinating ⁵ _____ function of the alphorn and its uses to call or calm ⁶ _____ have been lost.

Word Bank

herds	communicate	signal
efective	effective	hirds
diary	comunicate	single
cattle	cattles	dairy

 Listen. Pause. Say each sentence.

  MP3 J2-12G

Writing Practice

Write the words.

1 _____

adj powerful

2 _____

n cows

3 _____

n a group of animals such as cows or deer

4 _____

v have contact with

5 _____

n an action or sound to get someone's attention

6 _____

n a farm where milk and cheese are made

 Write the words in each blank.

Summary

The alphorn once had a _____ function in the mountains and villages of _____. It was mostly used by people who kept _____ herds to call or calm cows. Now it is mainly used at festivals or in _____.

Word Puzzle

 Complete the word puzzle.

1 ↓
cows

2 →
powerful

3 ↓
have contact with

4 ↓
a farm where milk and cheese are made

5 →
an action or sound to get someone's attention

6 →
a group of animals such as cows or deer

One Composer, Two Heads

Teacher's Book p.166

The famous Austrian composer Joseph Haydn died in 1809. Eight days after he died, two people took the head from his dead body. At the time, there was a common belief that the bumps in people's skulls could be "read." It was thought that "reading" the bumps in Haydn's head would reveal how the composer could write such beautiful music.

Eleven years after Haydn's death, an Austrian prince wanted to move Haydn's tomb to another place. It was then discovered that the composer's body had no head. Haydn's wig was there, but there was no skull. The prince was very angry, and searched for Haydn's skull. The thieves tricked the prince, giving him another skull that could go in Haydn's grave with the skeleton.

Decades later, in 1895, a music society in Vienna, Austria received a gift. It was Haydn's skull. Many decades after that, in 1954, Haydn's skull was placed together in the tomb with Haydn's skeleton. However, the other skull was left in the tomb, too, so there are now two skulls in Haydn's grave. But to whom does the other skull belong? It is a mystery in the world of classical music.

ANSWERS

UNIT 1
J2-1
p.11

- 1 (D) 2 (B) 3 (D) 4 (B) 5 (A) 6 (B) 7 (C) 8 (A) 9 (D) 10 (D)
- 1 sit-ups 2 injury 3 heels 4 cross 5 lower 6 strengthen
- 1 sit-up 2 injury 3 heel 4 cross your arms 5 lower 6 strengthen
- safe, sit-ups, strengthen, prevent
- → 3 sit-up 4 lower 5 heel ↓ 1 injury 2 cross your arms 3 strengthen

UNIT 2
J2-2
p.19

- 1 (A) 2 (C) 3 (B) 4 (B) 5 (A) 6 (B) 7 (A) 8 (B) 9 (D) 10 (D)
- 1 track 2 curves 3 sleds 4 made of 5 sturdy 6 skeleton
- 1 track 2 curve 3 sled 4 be made of 5 sturdy 6 skeleton
- Olympic, technology,metal, skeleton
- → 2 sturdy 3 sled 4 track ↓ 1 be made of 2 skeleton 5 curve

UNIT 3
J2-3
p.27

- 1 (A) 2 (A) 3 (A) 4 (D) 5 (C) 6 (C) 7 (A) 8 (C) 9 (B) 10 (B)
- 1 illegal 2 doping 3 prohibited 4 cheating 5 related 6 contracts
- 1 doping 2 illegal 3 be prohibited from 4 related to 5 cheating 6 contract
- drugs, reasons, athlete, cheating
- → 4 related to 6 illegal ↓ 1 cheating 2 be prohibited from 3 contract 5 doping

UNIT 4
J2-4
p.35

- 1 (A) 2 (A) 3 (D) 4 (C) 5 (C) 6 (C) 7 (C) 8 (D) 9 (D) 10 (D)
- 1 records 2 competition 3 high-performance 4 material 5 covered 6 banned
- 1 break a record 2 competition 3 high-performance 4 material 5 cover 6 ban
- broke, material, unfair, swimsuits
- → 4 break a record 6 ban ↓ 1 high-performance 2 cover 3 material 5 competition

UNIT 5
J2-5
p.45

- 1 (D) 2 (C) 3 (D) 4 (B) 5 (A) 6 (C) 7 (C) 8 (D) 9 (D) 10 (C)
- 1 techniques 2 lighting 3 landscape 4 location 5 costumes 6 waist
- 1 lighting 2 technique 3 landscape 4 location 5 costume 6 waist
- main, shot, full, filmmakers
- → 3 waist 4 lighting 5 technique ↓ 1 costume 2 landscape 4 location

UNIT 6
J2-6
p.53

- 1 (D) 2 (B) 3 (C) 4 (D) 5 (D) 6 (B) 7 (B) 8 (C) 9 (D) 10 (B)
- 1 collection 2 sculptures 3 used 4 palaces 5 fancy 6 decorated
- 1 collection of 2 sculpture 3 used to be 4 fancy 5 decorated 6 palace
- museums, buildings, million, world
- → 2 fancy 6 used to be ↓ 1 palace 3 sculpture 4 collection of 5 decorated

UNIT 7
J2-7
p.61

- 1 (C) 2 (C) 3 (B) 4 (C) 5 (A) 6 (D) 7 (C) 8 (B) 9 (C) 10 (B)
- 1 fine 2 wealthy 3 afford 4 feature 5 perspective 6 tiny
- 1 wealthy 2 fine 3 afford to do 4 feature 5 perspective 6 tiny
- paintings, Middle, time, because of
- → 2 wealthy 5 feature 6 fine ↓ 1 perspective 3 tiny 4 afford to do

UNIT 8
J2-8
p.69

- 1 (A) 2 (B) 3 (C) 4 (C) 5 (C) 6 (B) 7 (D) 8 (A) 9 (C) 10 (C)
- 1 mammals 2 reptiles 3 mascots 4 stands for 5 Cranes 6 monuments
- 1 mammal 2 reptile 3 mascot 4 crane 5 stand for 6 monument
- symbols, cranes, Korean, life
- → 3 stand for 5 crane 6 reptile ↓ 1 mascot 2 monument 4 mammal

UNIT 9
J2-9
p.79

- 1 (D) 2 (C) 3 (A) 4 (C) 5 (C) 6 (D) 7 (C) 8 (D) 9 (B) 10 (D)
- 1 claim 2 spoken 3 key 4 lyrics 5 clever 6 distinction
- 1 claim 2 spoken 3 key 4 lyrics 5 clever 6 distinction
- opera, between, lyrics, music
- → 3 claim 4 spoken 5 key ↓ 1 lyrics 2 distinction 3 clever

UNIT 10
J2-10
p.87

- 1 (A) 2 (D) 3 (D) 4 (D) 5 (A) 6 (A) 7 (B) 8 (C) 9 (B) 10 (B)
- 1 classical 2 composer 3 themes 4 audience 5 shocked 6 delighted
- 1 classical 2 composer 3 theme 4 audience 5 shocked 6 delighted
- poems, shocked, Seasons, classical
- → 1 composer 6 audience ↓ 2 shocked 3 classical 4 theme 5 delighted

UNIT 11
J2-11
p.95

- 1 (D) 2 (C) 3 (C) 4 (B) 5 (D) 6 (B) 7 (B) 8 (B) 9 (A) 10 (B)
- 1 symbols 2 end 3 volume 4 In addition 5 moderately 6 Interestingly
- 1 symbol 2 in addition 3 moderately 4 end with 5 volume 6 interestingly
- volume, quietly, loudly, moderately
- → 4 symbol 5 end with 6 in addition ↓ 1 interestingly 2 volume 3 moderately

UNIT 12
J2-12
p.103

- 1 (B) 2 (C) 3 (D) 4 (A) 5 (C) 6 (B) 7 (D) 8 (C) 9 (B) 10 (C)
- 1 effective 2 herds 3 communicate 4 dairy 5 signal 6 cattle
- 1 effective 2 cattle 3 herd 4 communicate with 5 signal 6 dairy
- signal, Europe, cattle, commercials
- → 2 effective 5 signal 6 herd ↓ 1 cattle 3 communicate with 4 dairy

엄선된 **100만 명**의 응시자 성적 데이터를 활용한 **AI기반** 데이터 공유 및 가치 고도화 **플랫폼**

TOSEL® Lab

공동기획　- 고려대학교 문과대학 언어정보연구소
　　　　　　- 국제토셀위원회

TOSEL Lab 이란?

국내외 15,000여 개 학교·학원 단체응시인원 중 엄선한 100만 명 이상의 실제 TOSEL 성적 데이터와, 정부(과학기술정보통신부)의 AI 바우처 지원 사업 수행기관 선정으로 개발된 맞춤식 AI 빅데이터 기반 영어성장 플랫폼입니다.

TOSEL Lab
지정교육기관 혜택

혜택 1
지역별 독점 사용권 부여

혜택 2
고려대학교 미래교육원
TOSEL 전문가 과정 입학특전

혜택 3
진로활동 참가특전

혜택 4
심층 성적분석자료 제공
학원 단체 성적분석자료 제공 / 개인별 고도화 성적분석자료 제공

혜택 5
시험고사장 자격부여

혜택 6
진단평가 기반
영어학습 컨텐츠 제공
Placement Test / Self Study / Monthly Test

혜택 7
시험 응시권 제공
시험 접수료 납부대신 응시권 사용
Placement Test 응시권 제공

학원장의 실질적인 비용부담 없이
TOSEL® Lab
브랜드를 사용할 수 있는 기회

TOSEL Lab 에는 어떤 콘텐츠가 있나요?

진단
맞춤형 레벨테스트로
정확한 평가 제공

응시자 빅데이터 분석에 기반한
테스트로 신규 상담 학생의
영어능력을 정확하게 진단하고
효과적인 영어 교육을 실시하기
위한 객관적인 가이드라인을
제공합니다.

교재
세분화된 레벨로
실력에 맞는 학습 제공

TOSEL의 세분화된 교재 레벨은
각 연령에 맞는 어휘와 읽기
지능 및 교과 과정과의 연계가
가능하도록 설계된 교재들로
효과적인 학습 커리큘럼을
제공합니다.

학습
다양한 교재연계 콘텐츠로
효과적인 자기주도학습

TOSEL 시험을 대비한 다양한
콘텐츠를 제공해 영어 학습에
시너지 효과를 기대할 수
있으며, 학생들의 자기주도
학습 습관을 더 탄탄하게 키울
수 있습니다.

Reading Series
내신과 **토셀 고득점**을 한꺼번에

[Pre-Starter] [Starter] [Basic] [Junior] [High-Junior]

- 각 단원 학습 도입부에 주제와 관련된 이미지를 통한 말하기 연습
- 각 Unit 별 4-6개의 목표 단어 제시, 그림 또는 영문으로 단어 뜻을 제공하여 독해 학습 전 단어 숙지
- 독해&실용문 연습을 위한 지문과 Comprehension 문항을 10개씩 수록하여 이해도 확인 및 진단
- 숙지한 독해 지문을 원어민 음성으로 들으며 듣기 학습 , 듣기 전, 듣기 중, 듣기 후 학습 커리큘럼 마련

Listening Series
한국 학생들에게 최적화된 듣기 실력 완성!

[Pre-Starter] [Starter] [Basic] [Junior] [High-Junior]

- 초등 / 중등 교과과정 연계 말하기&듣기 학습과 세분화된 레벨
- TOSEL 기출 문장과 실생활에 자주 활용되는 문장 패턴을 통해 듣기 및 말하기 학습
- 실제 TOSEL 지문의 예문을 활용한 실용적 학습 제공
- 실전 감각 향상과 점검을 위한 기출 문제 수록

Speaking Series
출간예정

Grammar Series

체계적인 단계별 **문법 지침서**

Pre-Starter | Starter | Basic | Junior | High-Junior

- 초등 / 중등 교과과정 연계 문법 학습과 세분화된 레벨
- TOSEL 기출 문제 연습과 최신 수능 출제 문법을 포함하여 수능 / 내신 대비 가능
- 이해하기 쉬운 그림, 깔끔하게 정리된 표와 설명, 다양한 문제를 통해 문법 학습
- 실전 감각 향상과 점검을 위한 기출 문제 수록

Voca Series

학년별 꼭 알아야하는 **단어 수록!**

Pre-Starter | Starter | Basic | Junior | High-Junior

- 각 단어 학습 도입부에 주제와 관련된 이미지를 통한 말하기 연습
- TOSEL 시험을 기준으로 빈출 지표를 활용한 예문과 문제 구성
- 실제 TOSEL 지문의 예문을 활용한 실용적 학습 제공
- 실전 감각 향상과 점검을 위한 실전 문제 수록

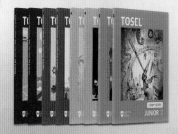

Story Series

읽는 재미에 실력까지 **동시에!**

Pre-Starter | Starter | Basic | Junior

- 초등 / 중등 교과과정 연계 영어 학습과 세분화된 레벨
- 이야기 지문과 단어를 함께 연결지어 학생들의 독해 능력을 평가
- 이해하기 쉬운 그림, 깔끔하게 정리된 표와 설명, 다양한 문제, 재미있는 스토리를 통한 독해 학습
- 다양한 단계의 문항을 풀어보고 학생들의 읽기, 듣기, 쓰기, 말하기 실력을 집중적으로 향상

교재를 100% 활용하는 TOSEL Lab 지정교육기관의 노하우!

Teaching Materials

TOSEL에서 제공하는 수업 자료로
교재 학습을 더욱 효과적으로 진행!

Study Content

철저한 자기주도학습 콘텐츠로
교재 수업 후 효과적인 복습!

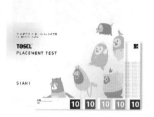

Test Content

교재 학습과 더불어 학생 맞춤형
시험으로 실력 점검 및 향상

100만 명으로 엄선된 **TOSEL**
성적 데이터로 탄생!

TOSEL Lab 지정교육기관을 위한 콘텐츠로
더욱 효과적인 수업을 경험하세요.

국제토셀위원회는 TOSEL Lab 지정교육기관에서 교재로
수업하는 학원을 위해 교재를 잘 활용할 수 있는 다양한
콘텐츠를 제공 및 지원합니다.

TOSEL Lab 지정교육기관은

국제토셀위원회 직속 TOSEL연구소에서 20년 동안 보유해온
전국 15,000여 개 교육기관 토셀 응시자들의 영어성적 분석데이터를
공유받아, 통계를 기반으로 한 전문적이고 과학적인 커리큘럼을 설계하고,
영어학습 방향을 제시하여,경쟁력있는 기관, 잘 가르치는 기관으로
해당 지역에서 입지를 다지게 됩니다.

TOSEL Lab 지정교육기관으로 선정되기 위해서는
소정의 심사 절차가 수반됩니다.

TOSEL Lab
심사신청

TOSEL Lab
더 알아보기

TOSEL° Lab